PUZZLE MASTERS

COLOUR QUEST

Buster Books

Puzzles by Lauren Farnsworth

Edited by Imogen Williams
Text by Amanda Learmonth
Designed by Derrian Bradder
Cover designed by Angie Allison and John Bigwood

First published in Great Britain in 2018 by Buster Books, an imprint of
Michael O'Mara Books Limited, 9 Lion Yard, Tremadoc Road, London SW4 7NQ

With material adapted from www.shutterstock.com

 www.mombooks.com/buster  Buster Books   @BusterBooks

ISBN: 978-1-78055-485-3

2 4 6 8 10 9 7 5 3

This book was printed and bound in June 2018
by Shenzhen Wing King Tong Paper Products Co. Ltd.,
Shenzhen, Guangdong, China

INTRODUCTION

Are you ready for the ultimate puzzle challenge?

This book is packed with extreme colouring puzzles – complete each one to reveal a hidden picture.

Each puzzle is a numbered pattern. Colour in the numbered spaces by following the colour code that appears on the page opposite. If there isn't a number in a space, leave it white. Gradually, a picture will be revealed.

Don't worry if you don't have pens and pencils in exactly the same shade as the colours shown. Get creative – make darker shades by pressing harder and blend colours together if you need to.

Beside each puzzle you will find four riddle-style clues to help you guess what picture you are going to reveal, with space underneath to write your answer.

Why not fill in how long each puzzle takes you to complete in the space provided at the bottom of the page?

The finished images and answers are all at the back of the book.

FUNNY FISH

I am a type of fish and you'll find me swimming in the warm shallow waters of the Indian and Pacific Oceans.

I often hide amongst sea anemones. Their poisonous tentacles, which don't sting me, protect me from hungry predators.

I am named for my brightly coloured stripes, and for the funny, wobbly way I swim.

I feed on tiny sea animals, called zooplankton, and small plants. I also keep sea anemones clean by picking harmful parasites from their tentacles.

WHAT AM I?

....

TIME: ....

1
2
3
4
5
6
7
8
9
10
11
12
13

NIGHT HUNTER

If you're lucky, you might spot me at dusk, swooping silently through the air in search of prey.

I am known for my wide-eyed stare and huge eyes at the front of my head. I also have a sharp, hooked beak.

Although my eyesight is excellent, I can't actually move my eyes. To look around, I can move my entire head almost in a full circle.

When hunting on a dark night, I use my super-sharp hearing to locate my prey. I can hear a mouse move from 20 metres away.

WHAT AM I?

....

TIME: ....

FAR, FAR AWAY

As the second largest planet in the Solar System, I am so huge you could fit 764 Earths inside me.

I lie billions of kilometres from Earth but can still be seen in the night sky as a bright point of light.

I am named after the Roman god of wealth and farming. There is also a day of the week that sounds like my name.

I am most well-known for the huge rings of ice crystals and dust that surround me.

WHAT AM I?

....

TIME: ....

1
2
3
4
5
6
7
8
9
10
11

NIBBLE AND GNAW

My slim, bendy body is perfect for running, jumping and climbing among the treetops.

I love to nibble on nuts and seeds. My four front teeth don't wear down from all the gnawing because they never stop growing.

Some of my species live on the ground. They collect nuts, fruit and seeds in their cheek pouches to store in burrows over winter.

You'll find me in all kinds of habitats, from rainforests and woodland to desert and bush.

WHAT AM I?

....

TIME: ....

1
2
3
4
5
6
7
8
9
10
11
12
13
14

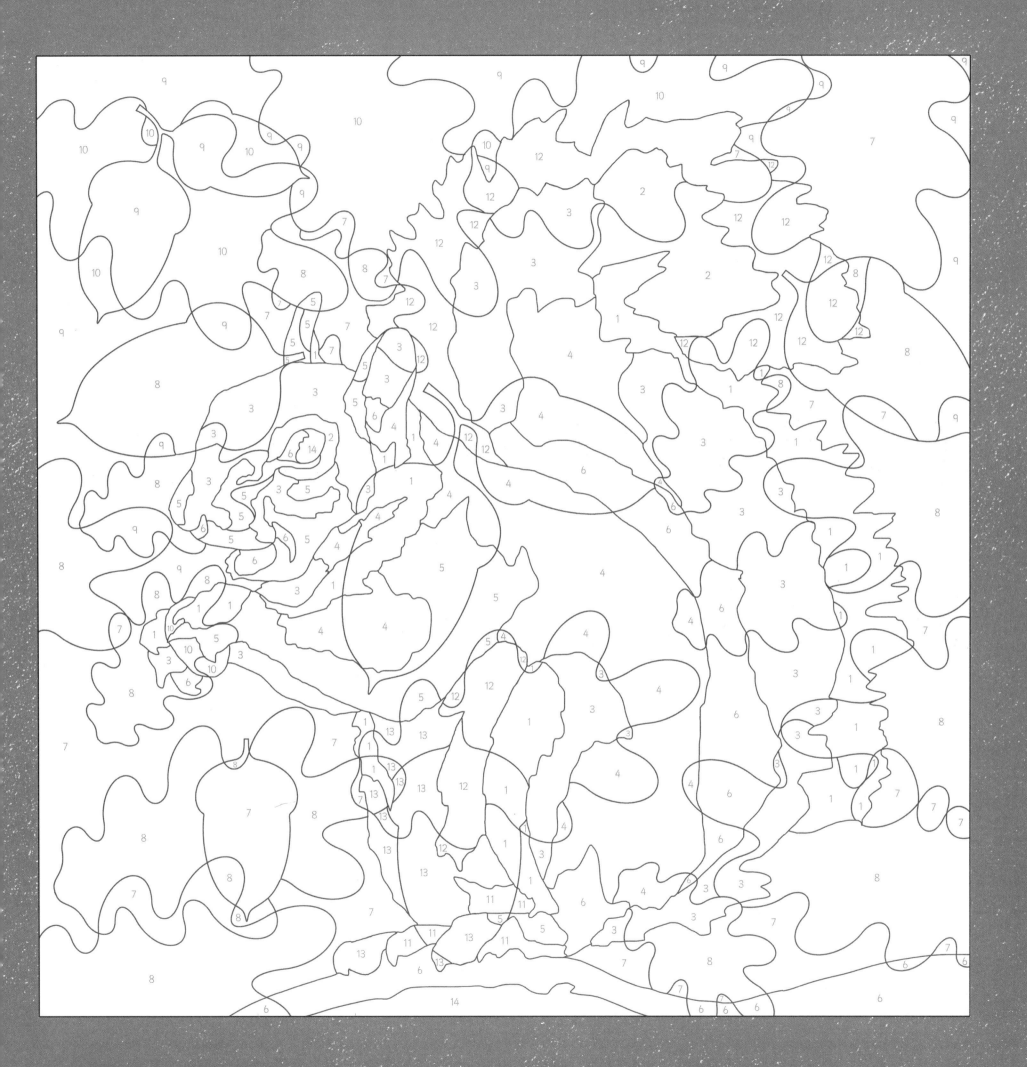

CLEVER CRITTER

With my large brain, I'm a clever creature. I have been known to use my long arms to unscrew the lid of a jam jar to get at the food inside.

I have long, powerful arms with rows of cup-shaped suckers. These help me to catch my prey and grip on to rocks on the seabed.

I live in seas and oceans around the world and belong to a group of animals called molluscs.

If another sea creature tries to attack me, I blast a cloud of black ink in its face to confuse it.

WHAT AM I?

....

TIME: ....

1
2
3
4
5
6
7
8
9
10
11
12
13

PRETTY IN PINK

I get my colouring from the plankton that I eat. They contain chemicals that turn my feathers pink.

My stilt-like legs are the longest of all birds. They keep me dry as I wade through the water in search of food.

I live in large flocks of thousands of birds in lakes and lagoons around the world.

I spend most of my day with my head upside down, filtering food from the water through my curved beak.

WHAT AM I?

....

TIME: ....

1
2
3
4
5
6
7
8
9
10
11
12
13

POWERFUL PREDATOR

I am the largest wild cat in the world. I can weigh up to 360 kilograms – that's about ten of you!

Unlike most other cats, I like the water. I'm a good swimmer and love to cool off in streams and lakes during the heat of the day.

The pattern on my fur camouflages me at night as I creep among the grasses in search of prey.

I live in Asia. Some of my subspecies include Amur, Malayan, Sumatran and Bengal.

WHAT AM I?

....

TIME: ....

1
2
3
4
5
6
7
8
9
10
11
12

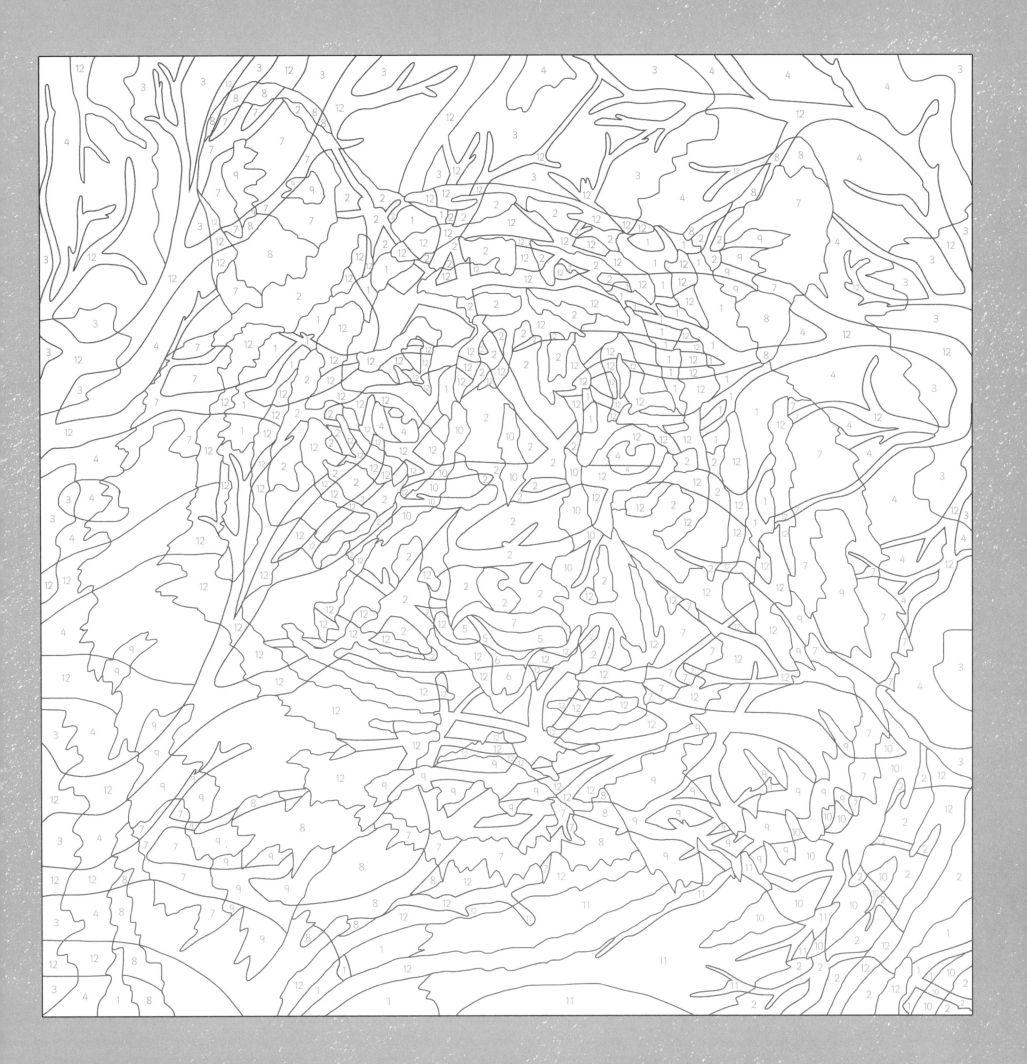

DART AND DIVE

I'm known for my fishing skills. When I spot my prey, I dive into the water, grab the fish in my long beak and dart back to my perch.

I live by slow-moving rivers and streams, where I dig nest burrows in the sandy soil.

I am about the size of an adult's hand. I need to eat my own body weight in fish each day to survive.

I have beautiful blue feathers on my back and wings. This makes me tricky to spot along the water's edge.

WHAT AM I?

....

TIME: ....

1
2
3
4
5
6
7
8
9
10
11
12
13
14

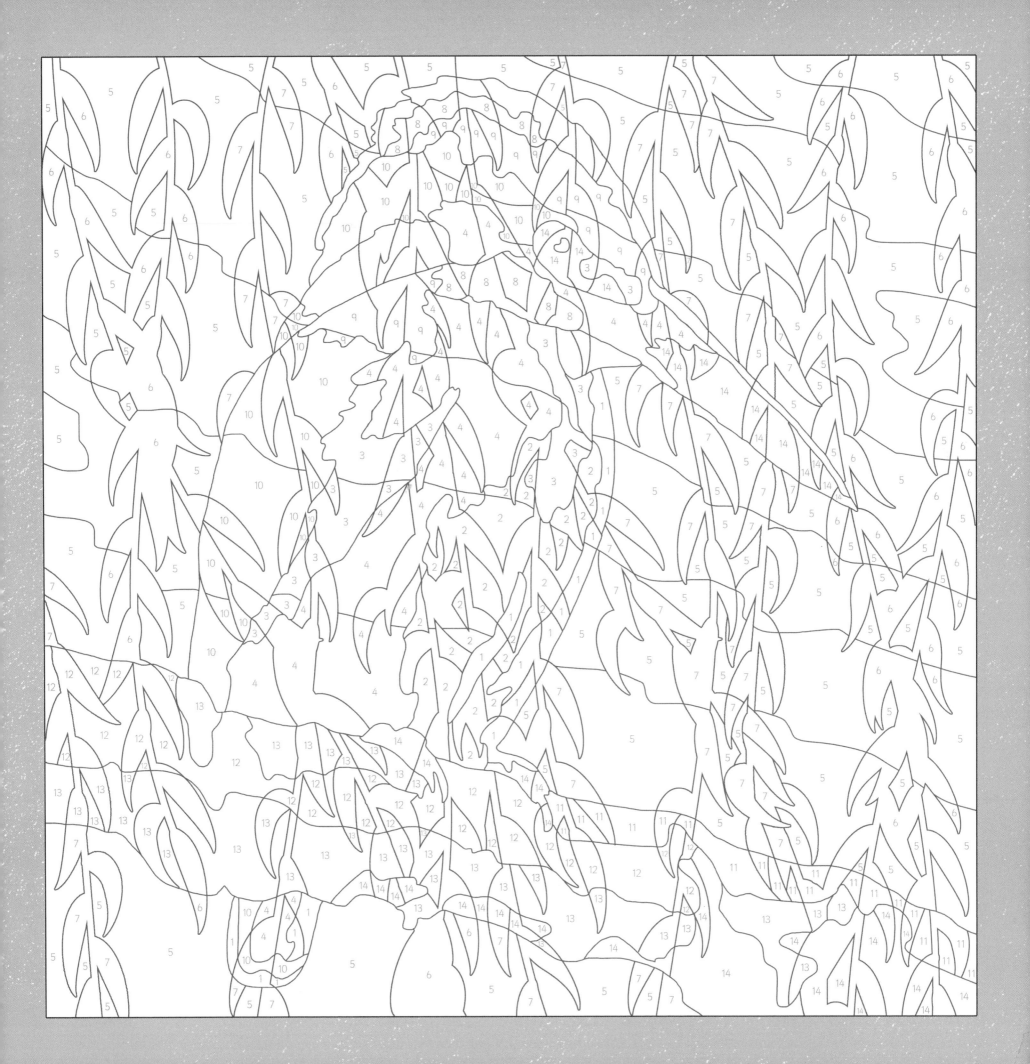

FLOWER POWER

1
2
3
4
5
6
7
8
9
10
11
12

I am a water plant with beautiful, cup-shaped flowers. I rise above the water on thick, leafless stalks.

One of my species is called 'sacred' and is found in tropical Asia and Australia. The colours of my petals are usually pink or white.

In some parts of Asia, my stalks are fried and sliced as chips, and my leaves are boiled to flavour tea.

In the Buddhist and Hindu religions, I symbolize beauty and purity.

WHAT AM I?

....

TIME: ....

MAKING TRACKS

I whizz through cities, countryside, along mountain sides and deep under ground. The fastest I can travel is a speedy 603 kilometres an hour.

I have been a popular form of transport since the 19th century.

Back in the 1800s, my different parts included a firebox, piston, cylinders and a steam pipe.

I used to be powered by coal or wood, but nowadays I mostly run on diesel or electricity.

WHAT AM I?

....

1
2
3
4
5
6
7
8
9
10
11
12

TIME: ....

CHANGING COLOURS

I'm a tree-dwelling lizard with a long tail and grasping feet that hold tightly on to the branches.

My eyes move separately to each other, so I can look around for prey without moving my head.

My skin can change colour depending on my body temperature or how I'm feeling. If I'm frightened or angry, I may change from green to yellow.

In less than a second, I can shoot out my sticky tongue, snatch an insect and snap it back in again.

WHAT AM I?

....

1
2
3
4
5
6
7
8
9
10
11
12

TIME: ....

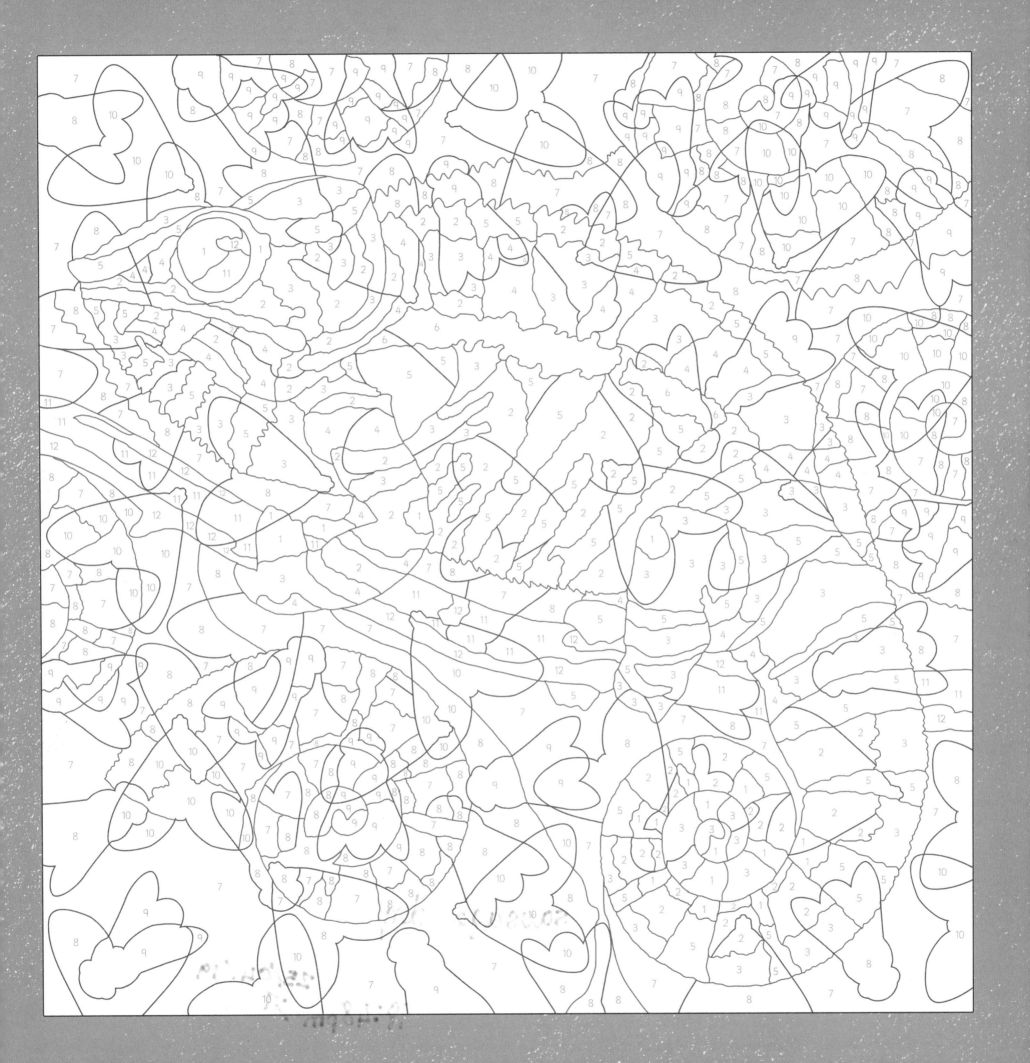

TINY BUT TOUGH

With my short legs and long body I look a bit like a sausage, which is how I got my nickname.

My name means 'badger dog' in German. I was originally bred to hunt badgers and other tunnelling animals, such as foxes.

I make a loving, playful pet. I like to be the centre of attention and need plenty of cuddles.

I might be small but I'm also tough and brave. I have large paws for digging and a strong, barrel-like chest.

1
2
3
4
5
6
7
8
9
10
11
12

WHAT AM I?

.....sausage dog.....

25/04/19

TIME: 18:48 pm

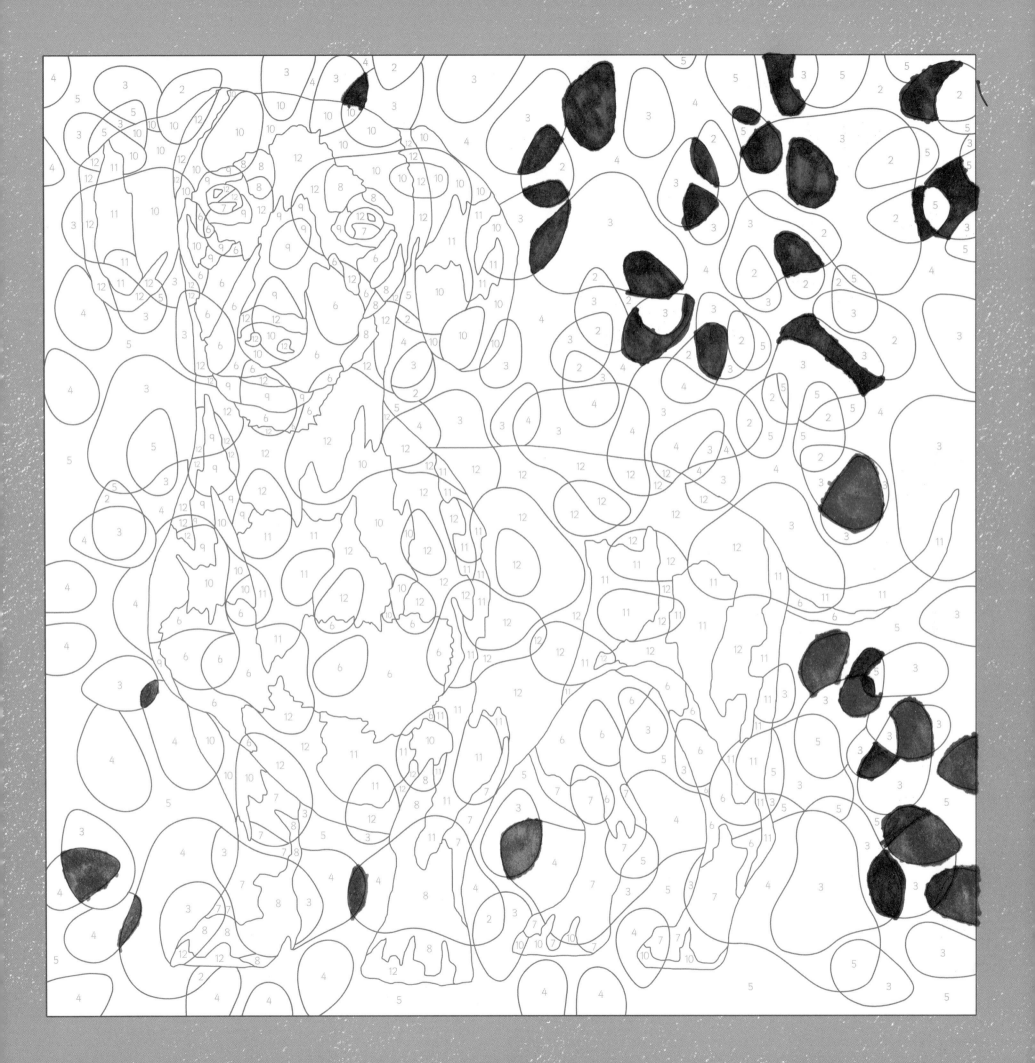

BRILLIANTLY BRIGHT

My squawks can be heard echoing through the Amazonian canopy. I use my calls to communicate with others in my flock.

I use my strong toes to climb through the branches of my colourful rainforest home.

My brightly-coloured feathers make me harder to spot among the colourful forest trees.

My beak is so powerful that I can easily crack nuts and seeds with it in one crunch.

1
2
3
4
5
6
7
8
9
10
11
12
13
14

WHAT AM I?

....

TIME: ....

FINE FORTRESS

1
2
3
4
5
6
7
8
9
10

Within my walls you might find a great hall, solar, keep and bailey. You may also once have seen pages, jesters and minstrels.

I am made from stone or wood. My walls and towers are tall and strong to protect against attackers.

I am the fortified home of a king or lord who lived hundreds of years ago.

Many of us were built during the Middle Ages, between the 5th and 15th centuries, around Europe and the Middle East.

WHAT AM I?

....

TIME: ....

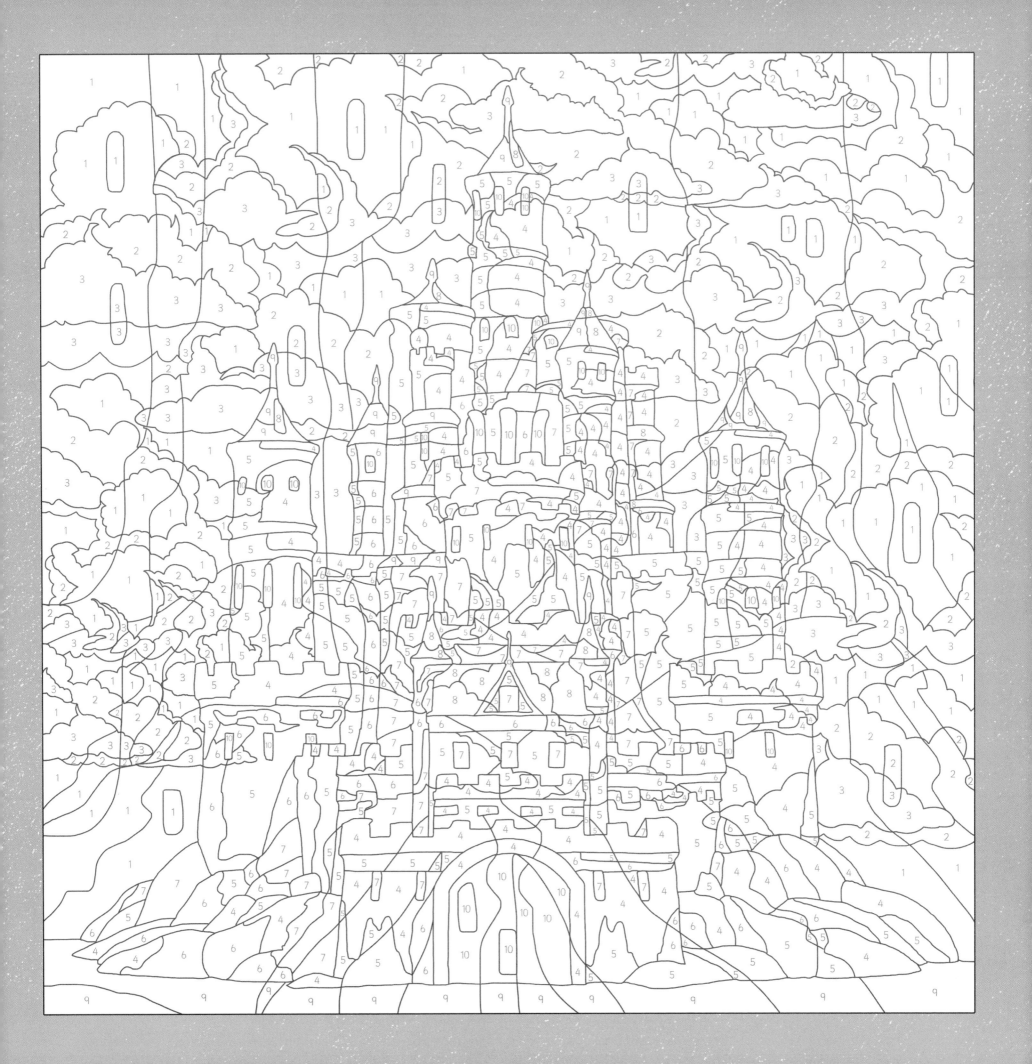

BIRDS OF A FEATHER

I'm a member of the cockatoo family but I'm slightly smaller. I grow to about 32 centimetres long.

You can recognize me from the feathery crest on top of my head. My crest raises and lowers depending on my mood.

You'll find me in the forests of Australia, flying around in huge flocks and roosting in tree hollows.

I am a sociable bird and enjoy spending time with others of my kind.

WHAT AM I?

....

TIME: ....

1
2
3
4
5
6
7
8
9
10
11
12
13
14
15
16
17

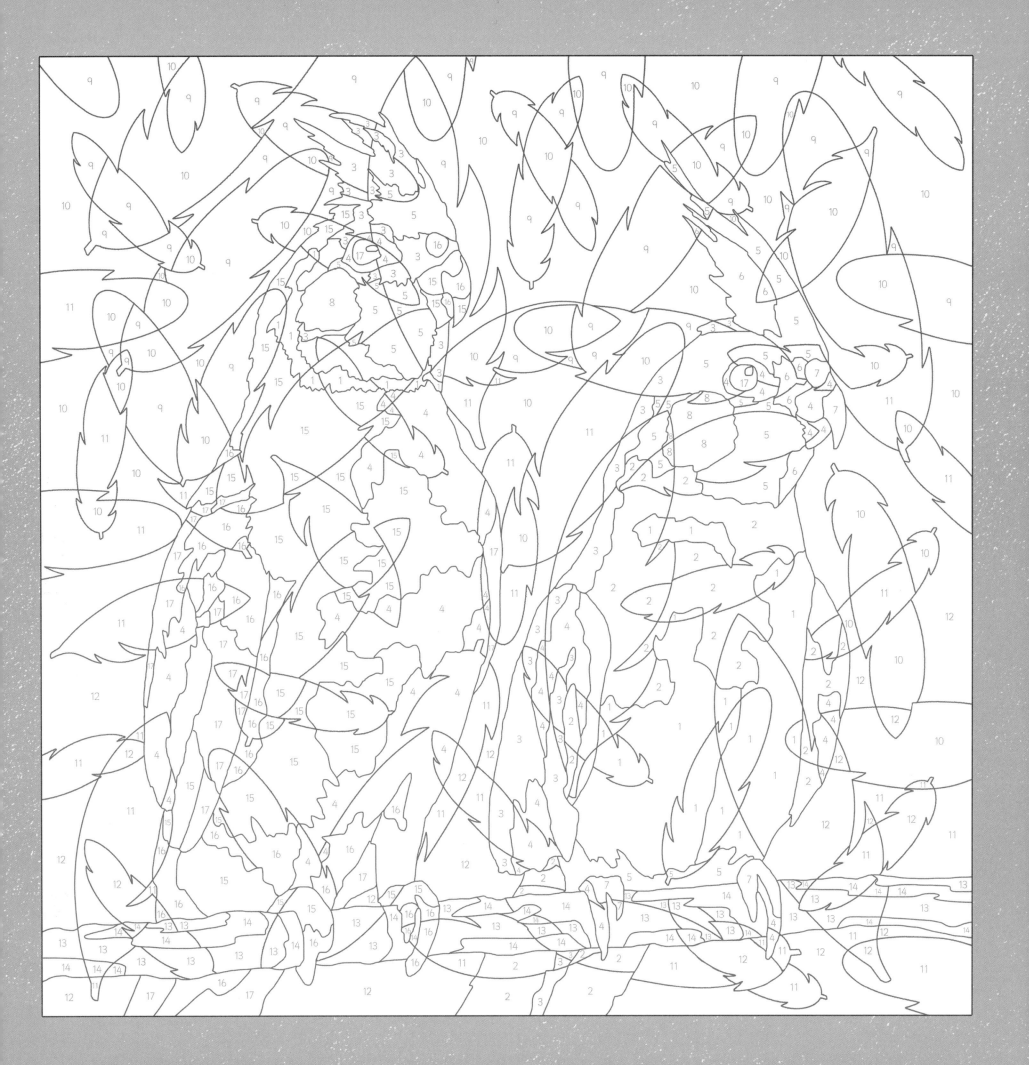

PAINTED LADY

I am always beautifully presented, with neat hair, exquisite clothes and delicate make-up.

I perform tea ceremonies in a special building called a tea house.

I wear a traditional Japanese gown called a kimono, embroidered with detailed patterns.

I am an expert at singing and dancing, flower arranging and calligraphy. In Japanese, my name means 'art person'.

WHAT AM I?

....

TIME: ....

1
2
3
4
5
6
7
8
9
10
11
12
13
14
15

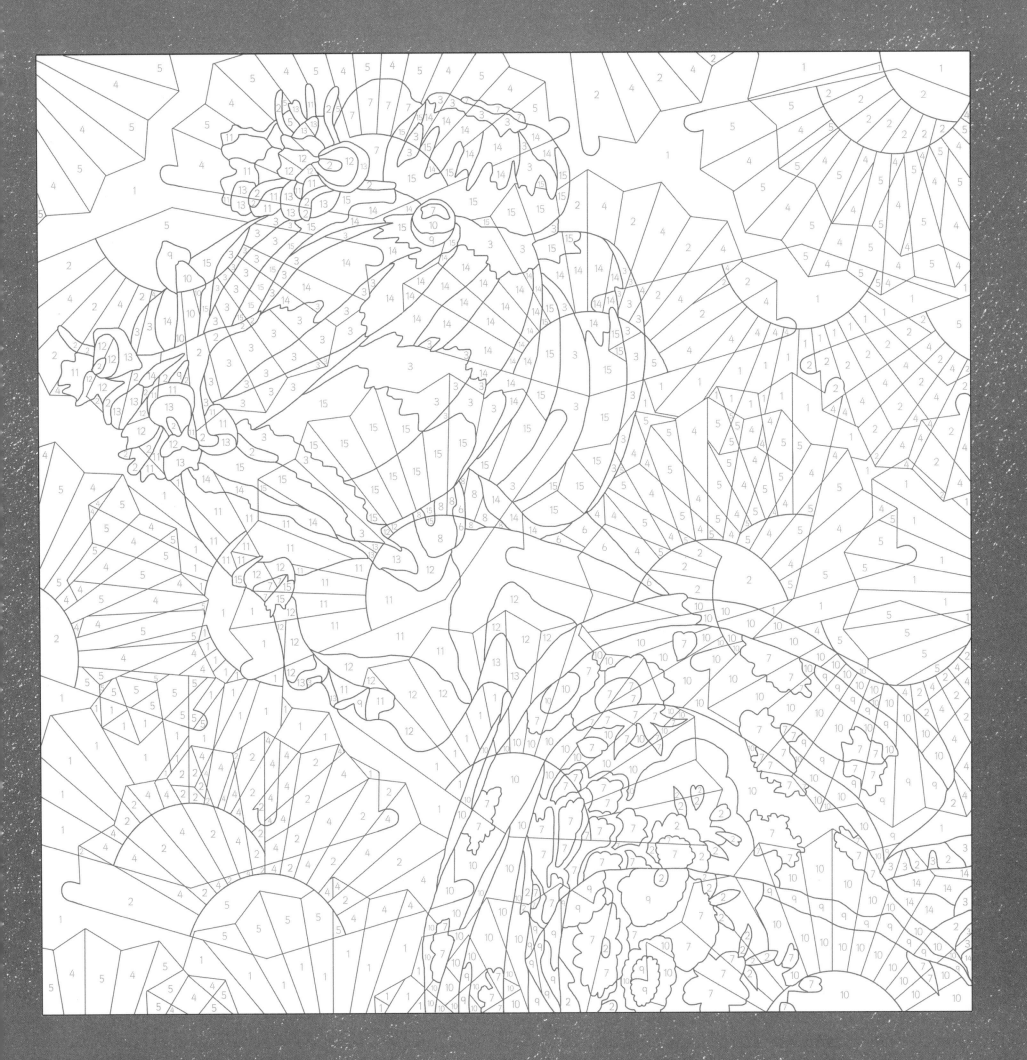

SPLASHING ABOUT

1
2
3
4
5
6
7
8
9
10
11
12

I live in rivers and seas around the world, but I'm not a fish. I have a long, furry body, short legs and webbed feet.

I love to munch on fish and other water animals, such as crabs. Sometimes I'll gobble up frogs, insects, snakes and lizards.

My body is long, slim and supple to help me twist and turn in the water as I chase after my prey. My thick, water-repellent fur keeps me warm in the chilly waters.

You might spot me splashing and playing about in the water, or floating on my back as I take a little rest.

WHAT AM I?

....

TIME: ....

TALL TOWER

I am a tower-like structure made of stone, wood or brick. I have many levels and a curved roof.

I was built mainly for religious worship, or for storing precious sacred objects.

I can mostly be found in the countries of Eastern and Southeastern Asia, such as India, China and Japan.

I am sometimes used as a decorative building in gardens and parks.

WHAT AM I?

....

TIME: ....

COOL AND CAMOUFLAGED

1
2
3
4
5
6
7
8

You will find me in the grasslands and treeless savannahs of East and Southern Africa.

Each of us has a unique pattern of stripes, much like your fingerprints. Underneath my dazzling stripes, my skin is actually all black.

As a herbivore, I love to munch on the local flora of my home, such as grass, shrubs and even bark.

Being a member of the horse family, I communicate through braying and neighing.

WHAT AM I?

....

TIME: ....

GIGANTIC JAWS

I'm a huge mammal with an incredibly wide mouth. My enormous teeth can grow up to 50 centimetres long.

I spend most of my days keeping cool in the rivers and lakes of Africa. My love of water is where I get my name, which means 'river horse' in Greek.

My eyes and ears are on top of my head. This means I can look and listen out for danger while the rest of me is submerged in the water.

Despite my size, I'm a good swimmer. I can hold my breath underwater for up to 5 minutes.

WHAT AM I?

....

1
2
3
4
5
6
7
8
9
10
11
12
13

TIME: ....

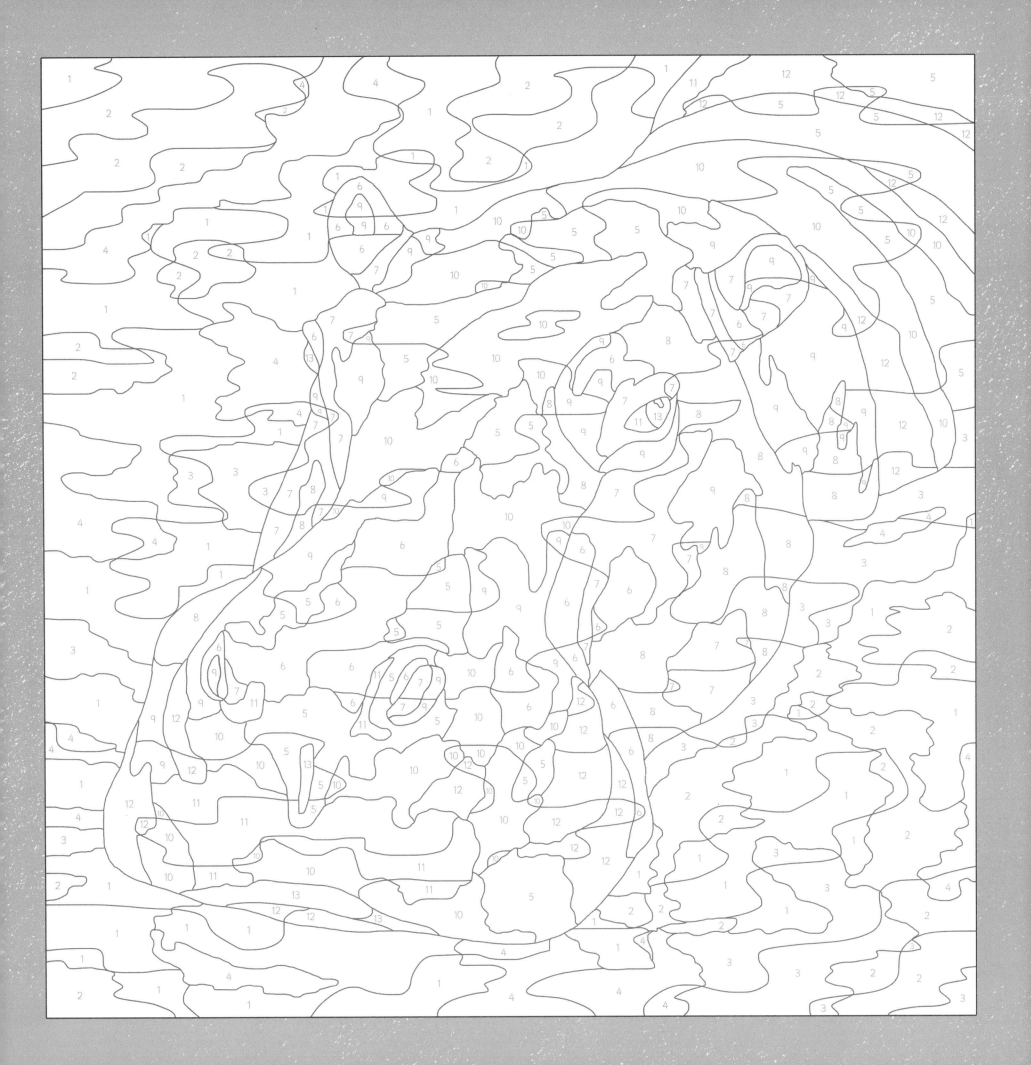

SNAP, SNAP!

1
2
3
4
5
6
7
8
9
10
11
12
13

I am not a crocodile or an alligator, but I belong to a group of reptiles called crocodilians. My name means 'alligator' in Spanish.

You'll find me in Central and South America, lurking in groups along riverbanks and swamps.

I am usually smaller than my alligator and crocodile relatives, but my bite is just as fierce.

I have a long, rounded snout, beady eyes and a huge tail. My jaw is powerful to help me kill my prey, such as fish, birds and small animals.

WHAT AM I?

....

TIME: ....

FURRY FRIEND

I'm a small, furry rodent, also known as a cavy. I have a rounded body, short legs and no tail.

I come from the grasslands of South America, where I was first bred by humans for food. Now I make a popular pet.

I don't come from the country in my name, and I'm not related to the animal my name suggests.

I 'chat' with my friends using all sorts of sounds, including squeaks, chirps, whistles and purrs.

WHAT AM I?

....

TIME: ....

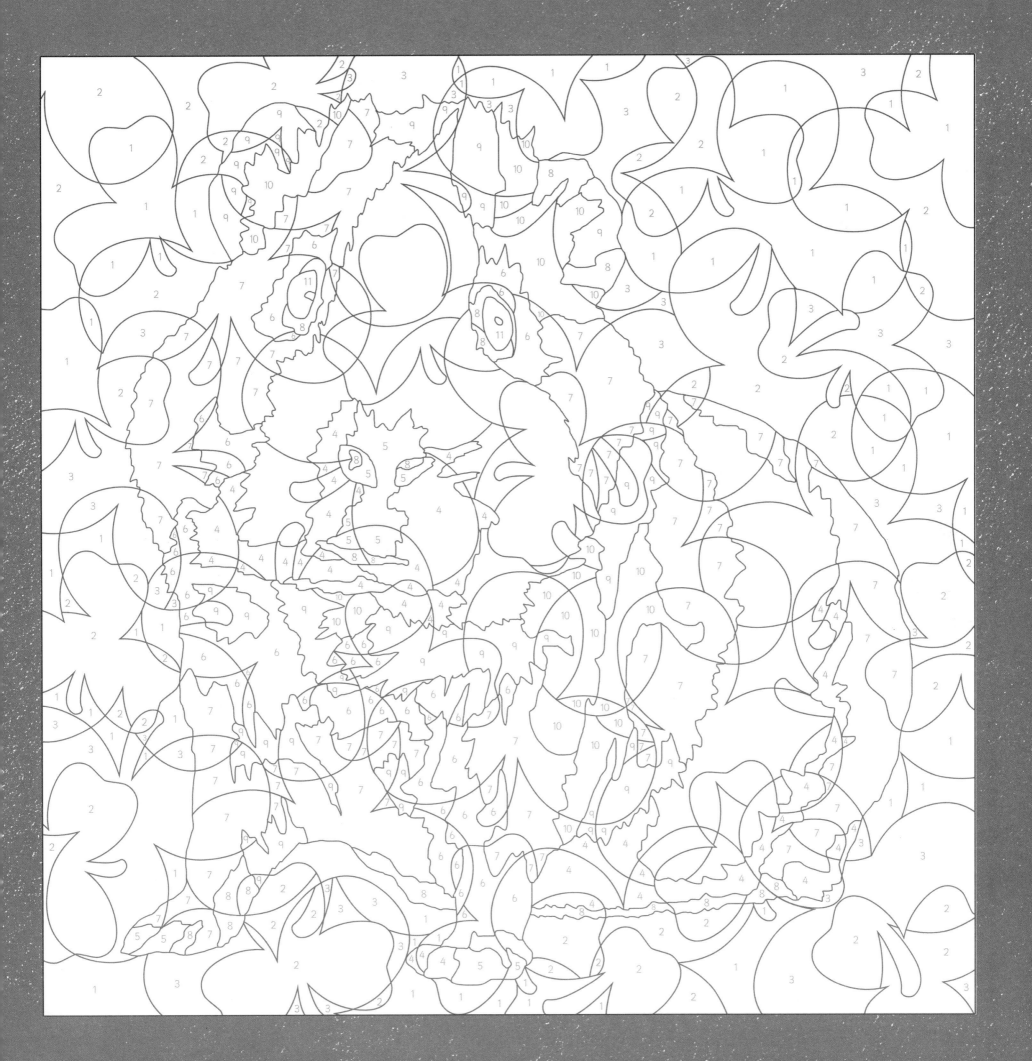

SMALL AND SPINY

I might not look like one, but I'm actually a fish. I am named for the unusual shape of my head.

My body is covered in tiny, spiny plates. I use my curved tail to grip on to sea plants and wait for passing prey.

To keep me safe from predators, I'm a master of camouflage. I can quickly change my colour to match my surroundings.

I'm one of the few animals on Earth whose male gives birth to the young.

WHAT AM I?

....

TIME: ....

1
2
3
4
5
6
7
8
9
10
11
12
13
14

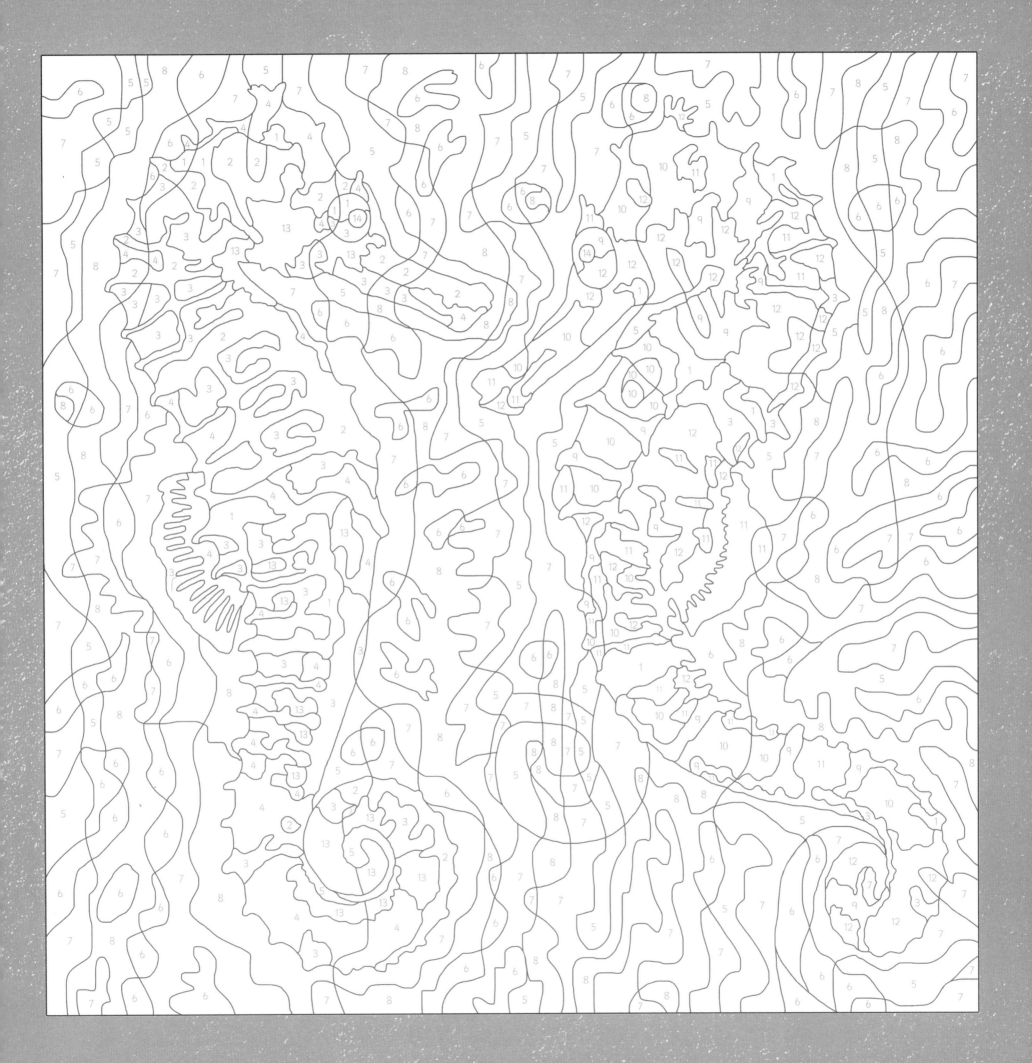

ON THE ROAD

For more than 130 years I have been giving people the freedom to travel where and when they like.

My first petrol-powered model travelled at a top speed of 16 kilometres an hour. Nowadays, I can reach speeds of over 300 kilometres an hour.

I am made mostly from steel, aluminium and plastic. My different parts include a bonnet, engine, fuel tank and exhaust pipe.

I am an important means of transport for emergency services, such as the police and paramedics.

WHAT AM I?

....

TIME: ....

1 2 3 4 5 6 7 8 9 10 11 12 13 14

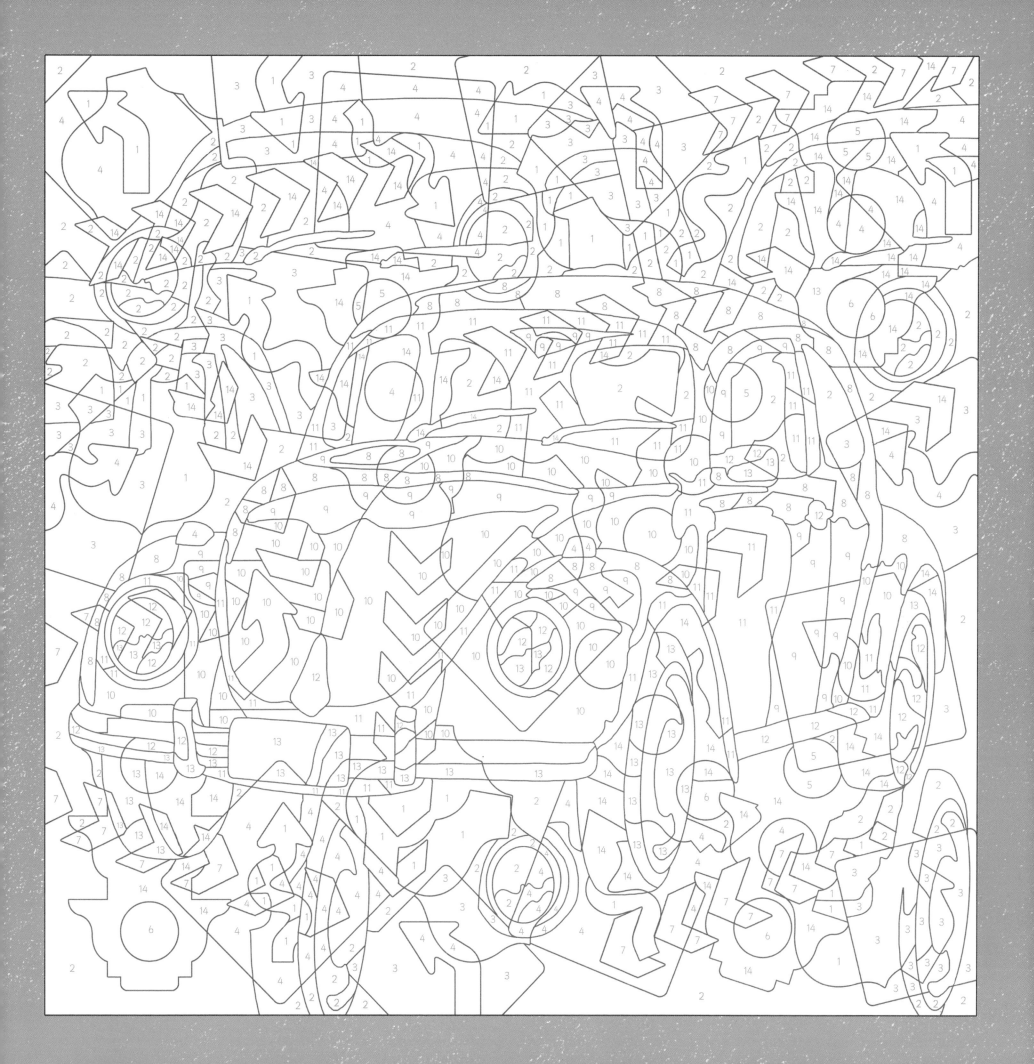

SEEING SPOTS

With my beautiful spotted coat, long whiskers and tail, I am easy to recognize.

I am strong enough to drag prey twice my size up into the trees, where I can keep it hidden away from other predators.

You'll find me in Africa and Asia, but my numbers are decreasing in the wild, due to deforestation and hunting.

I like to spend my time up in the trees. Hidden by the leaves, I can stalk my prey from above, then pounce down on it.

WHAT AM I?

....

TIME: ....

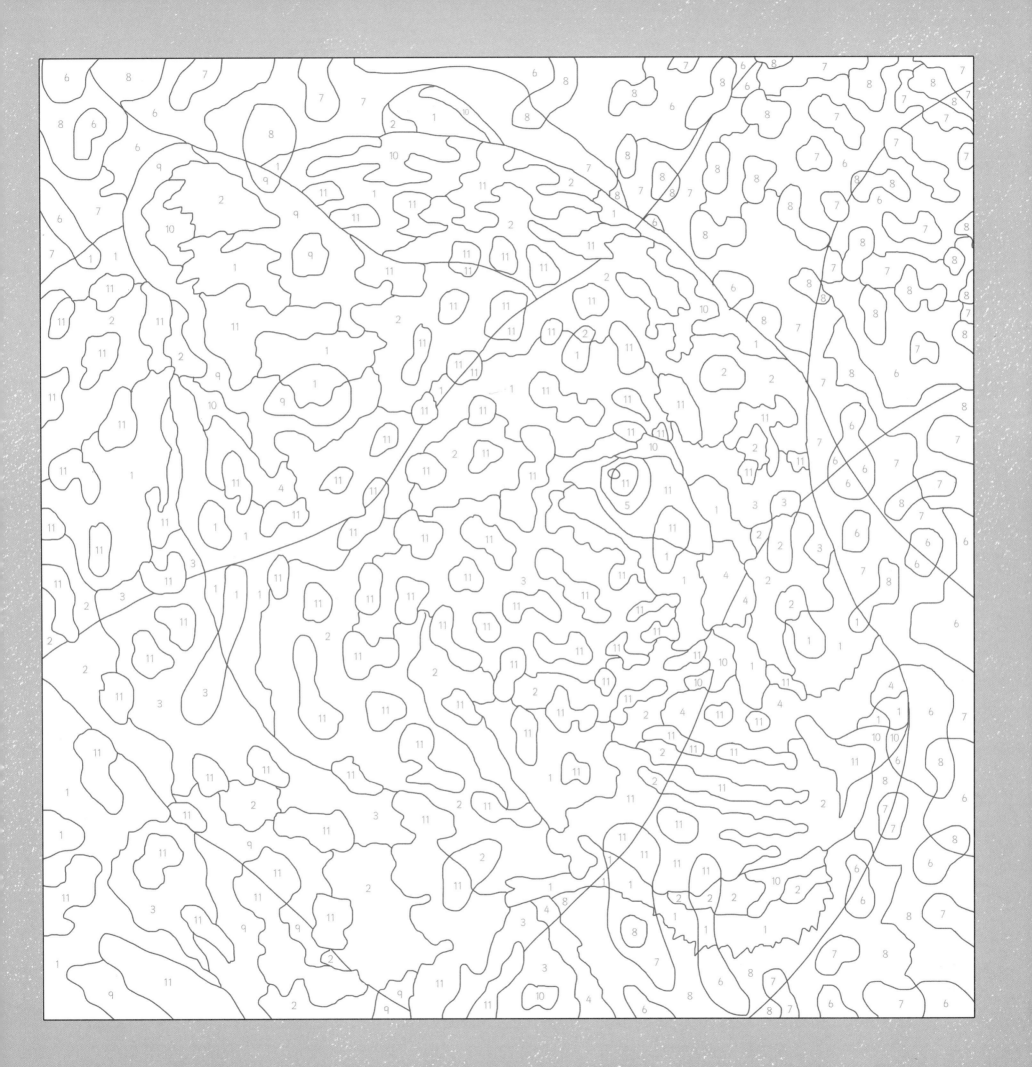

CUTE CLIMBER

1
2
3
4
5
6
7
8
9
10
11
12

I live in the foothills of the Himalayan mountains in Asia, where I spend most of my time up in the trees.

I am about the size of a large pet cat, with rust-coloured fur and special claws that help me climb skilfully from tree to tree.

Scientists used to think I was a kind of bear or raccoon, but now they say I'm not closely related to any other animal.

Like another animal of a similar name, my favourite food is bamboo. I'll also happily munch on other grasses, fruit and birds' eggs.

WHAT AM I?

....

TIME: ....

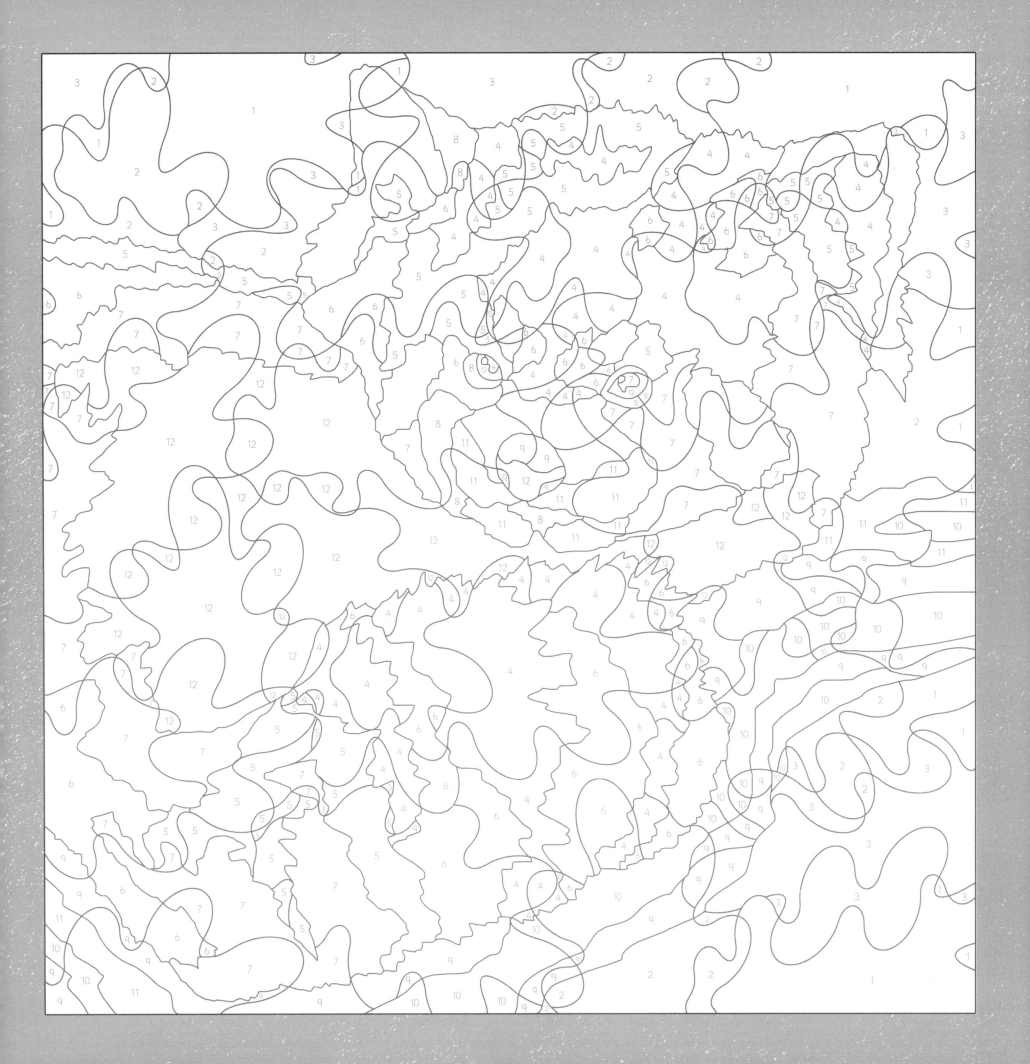

BILLIONS OF BUGS

The group of insects to which I belong is the largest in the world. Out of every three insects, one will be like me.

I have long, delicate flying wings that fold up beneath a pair of tough, hard outer wings.

There are at least 400,000 species of me. I'm found all over the world, in every type of habitat, from rainforest to desert.

My size varies hugely. I can be as tiny as a full stop or as large as an adult's hand.

WHAT AM I?

....

TIME: ....

1
2
3
4
5
6
7
8
9
10
11
12
13

HIGH FLYERS

1
2
3
4
5
6
7
8
9
10
11
12
13

My first successful launch was in 1903 by the Wright brothers. I stayed in the air for 59 seconds.

My different parts include the fuselage, cockpit, wheels, and propellers.

I have a tail and wings, but I'm not a bird.

I vary in size, and can be as small as a school bus or as huge as eight buses put together.

WHAT AM I?

....

TIME: ....

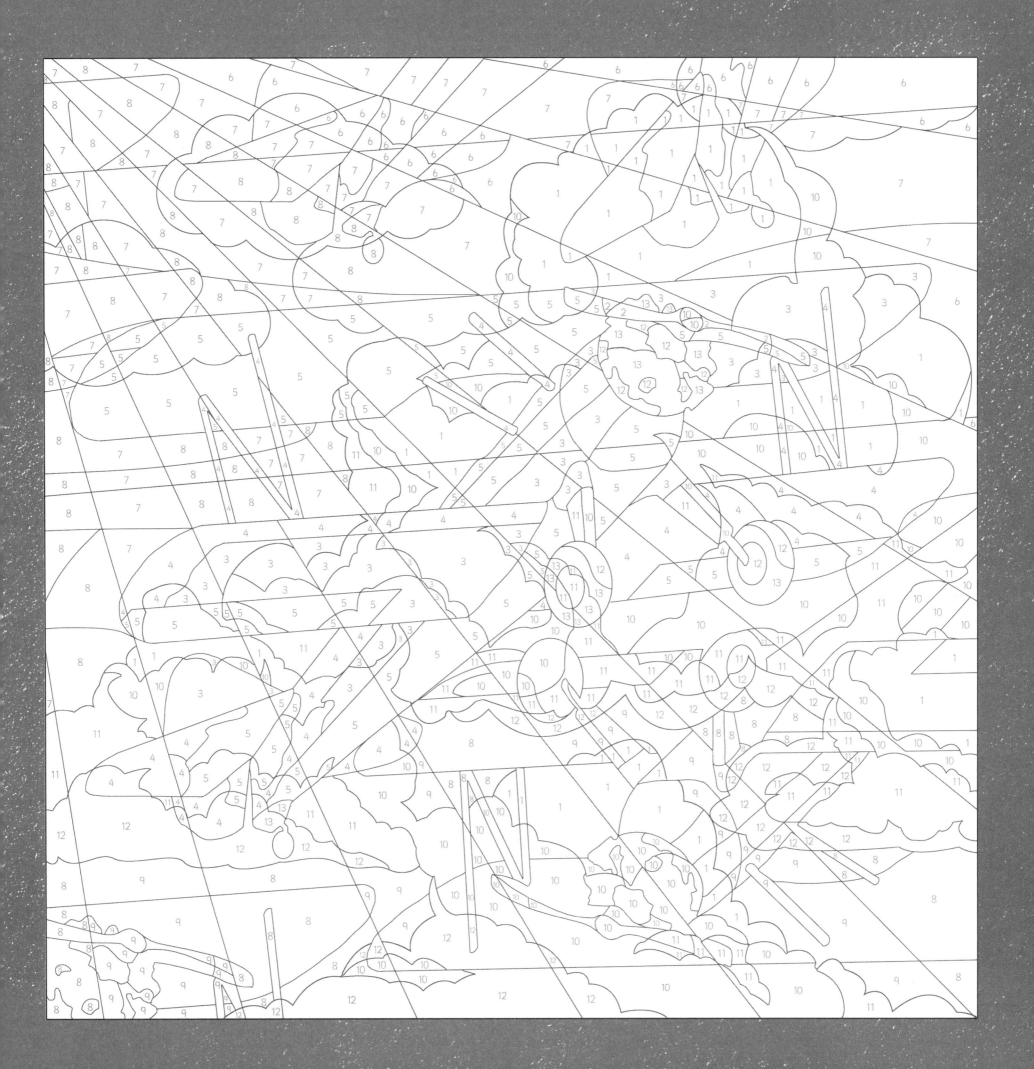

SCUTTLE AND SHUFFLE

1
2
3
4
5
6
7
8
9
10
11
12

I belong to a group of animals called decapods, which means 'ten legs'. Others in my group include prawns and shrimps.

There are around 7,000 species of me around the world. Many of us have funny names, such as hermit, spider, robber, ghost and fiddler.

I use my sharp pincers for catching and picking apart my prey. I also use them for fighting off predators.

As I grow, my hard shell begins to split open and fall off. The new, softer shell underneath expands before it hardens.

WHAT AM I?

....

TIME: ....

ALL THE ANSWERS

1 CLOWN FISH

2 OWL

3 SATURN

4 SQUIRREL

5 OCTOPUS

6 FLAMINGO

7 TIGER

8 KINGFISHER

9 LOTUS FLOWER

10 TRAIN

11 CHAMELEON

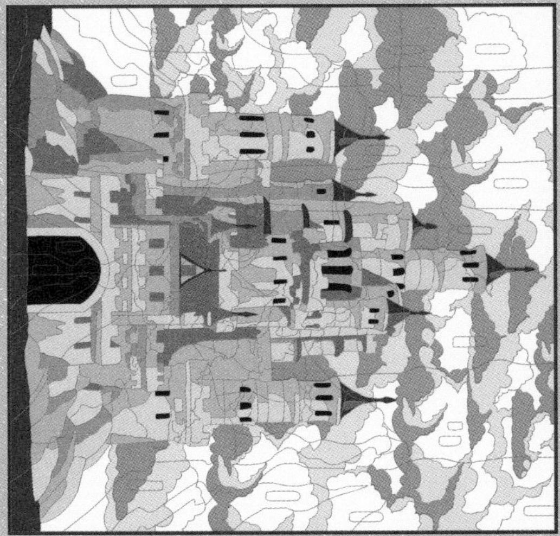

12 DACHSHUND (SAUSAGE DOG)

13 PARROT

14 CASTLE

15 COCKATIELS

16 GEISHA

17 OTTER

18 PAGODA

19 ZEBRA

20 HIPPOPOTAMUS

21 CAIMAN

22 GUINEA PIG

23 SEAHORSES

24 CAR

25 LEOPARD

26 RED PANDA

27 BEETLE

28 AEROPLANE

29 CRAB